Berlin. 30 years after Wall, the city continues to rein capital is a perfect cocktail of arts scene, lush green spaces and the famous free spirit that turned it into a bohemian wonderland long ago.

But the abandon of the post-Wall era has given way to a newfound cosmopolitanism. And the food panorama is evolving apace, with Michelin-starred chefs joining street food mavericks and adventurous kitchens channeling the continent's best ideas.

Each neighbourhood has its own personality—from upscale Charlottenburg with its Asian quarter to arty gentrified Kreuzberg and rough-around-the-edges Neukölln, where industrial spaces are being transformed into nodes of culture.

Here, some local heroes share their side of the city. An undisputed pioneer of the 1990s club scene, a woman at the vanguard of the fashion world, an artist and publisher couple, a top restaurateur and one of the city's edgiest curators. A feature evokes a childhood beside the Wall, a photographic showcase recalls the grim, glitzy 1980s and an original short story crackles through a seedy nightscape. Get lost in the sights, sounds and flavours of the city. Get lost in Berlin.

"Only an idea has the power to spread so widely" said Mies van der Rohe, third and last director of the Bauhaus. And despite lasting only 14 years, the art, architecture and design college was perhaps the most influential of the 20th century. Its founder Martin Gropius made the initial designs which eventually became the *Bauhaus-Archiv*. Sitting on the Landwehr Canal, the museum teaches the history of the movement and displays works from seminal teachers including Gropius, van der Rohe, Paul Klee and Wassily Kandinsky.
• Bauhaus-Archiv, Klingelhöferstrasse 14, Tiergarten, bauhaus.de

Originally a Weimar-era department store, the building Soho House occupies has weathered some of Berlin's darkest moments to emerge victorious. Today, it represents the city's outward-looking ethos. Nowhere more so than its on-site retail paradise *The Store*. From records and books to clothes and furniture, it features brands like Balenciaga and Raf Simons among limited-edition collaborations. The Store Kitchen provides coffee and juices to sip from couches, along with healthy breakfasts and lunches.

• The Store, Soho House, Torstrasse 1, Mitte, sohohouseberlin.com

From Left-Field Downtempo to Thespian Schnitzel

Symphony of a Metropolis

What's a jaded clubber to do when tired of all the classic Berlin floors? Take it down a few BPMs, that's what. In Friedrichshain, Berghain's sub-club *Säule* offers slow jams to vary from the thump of the turbine hall. Meanwhile, a hidden Mitte dance hall offers a supreme sound system and a broken-in wooden floor for seasoned dancers' feet. *Beate Uwe* (pictured) is open weekends, with regular label showcases plus left-field names. Sunday's "Something Slow" parties offer the downtempo sound that's seeped into Berlin since Atonal Festival's return.

• Various locations

Photos: 1) JD, 2) Udo Siegfriedt, 3) KW Institute for Contemporary Art

Art by the Yard

Galleries mushroomed in Mitte's Scheunenviertel after the fall of the Wall. The situation was prime: exquisite GDR buildings stood in states of uncertain ownership, ready to be transformed by clever creators. It was in an old margarine factory where a group of artists hatched the long-running space now known as KW Institute for Contemporary Art. The curators decided to eschew a permanent collection, thanks to the belief that a changing programme would allow them to stay responsive to an art world that's constantly in flux. Stop in to have your artistic sensibilities primed by anything from installations, paintings and videos to sculptures—or all of the above. In fact, the shows vary so wildly that the entire layout of the five-floor space is transformed for each one. KW's friendly courtyard, complete with Dan Graham's glass box bar, encapsulates the open-minded ethos of the institution—and is beautiful in every season.

• KW Institute for Contemporary Art, Auguststrasse 69, Mitte, kw-berlin.de

Easy Like Sunday Mitte

Billy Wilder's "Menschen am Sonntag" (1930), is set in an unhurried Berlin. We see the city centre on the last day of the week—slowed-down and drawn out. In stark contrast to its normally hyperkinetic vibes, Sunday remains a wonderfully peaceful day to visit Mitte. Forget the shopping and go for a canal-side stroll to work up an appetite. Sunday brunch at *House of Small Wonder* (pictured) is always a good idea—not least because of the kitchen's American-Franco-Japanese mix of influences. Go for the Okinawan taco rice or croissant French toast and wash it all down with a creamy matcha latte. The beautiful interior is just as pleasing—and insta-worthy. If you're more of a late starter, *Lokal* is an excellent bet for a Sunday feast crafted entirely from local produce. Options might include saddle of Brandenburg boar or cod cheeks, and there's always veggie options too. The off-menu shareable côte de boeuf comes recommended—order it when booking your table, ahead of time.

• Mitte, various locations

Night Ladies and Luvvies

When a heavyweight boxer opens a restaurant-bar in the 1950s that packs in the theatre crowd, and stays alive until now—you know something very right is going on. *Diener Tattersall* (pictured) is as fine for schnitzel as for endless schnapps, and the hanging photos of long-gone thespians will keep you company until the real ones turn up. Follow the theatrical thread round the corner to the lady who greets at *Bar Zentrale*. Under the tracks this roomy, well-lit bar has crisp cocktails to match the acid glamour of the hostess.

• Charlottenburg, various locations

Photos: 1) House of Small Wonders, 2) Uho, 3) Lienhard Schulz, 4) UH

Outdoor | See for Yourself

Forget the concrete. Berlin has around 80 natural bodies of water swimmable during hot months, and as picturesque in winter. Many offer sandy beaches, water sports, boating and more; plus areas where you'll come face to... face with some very unembarrassed nudists. For remoter lakes you need a car. But public transport reaches some equally breathtaking spots. For example, a public bus brings you to *Tegeler See* in the northwest.

Berlin's second largest lake has an old-school, residential charm, often garnished by currywurst and beer stands at several public beaches. It holds seven islands—a ferry reaches three of them and a steamboat offers a circuit. At its north end find the city's oldest oak tree, 900-year-old "Fat Marie". Or just relax with a beer for one of Berlin's most heart-melting sunsets.
• Tegeler See, Tegel

Food | Asian Strip

Eastern delights line Charlottenburg's famous Kantstrasse—but don't go on appearances. *Lon Men's Noodle House* might boast no frills, but the authentic Taiwanese dumplings, beef soup and homemade noodles transcend the décor. For a more plush—and pricey—experience, cross the street to *893 Ryotei* (pictured). Hidden behind a questionable façade, its marble countertops laden with inventive Nikkei cuisine await. For another upscale option, *Dao* does Thai the right way, meaning bubbling curries with the spice levels turned way up. Just down the road, *Papaya* offers an excursion to Thailand's northern extremes by way of tom yam soup and duck salad.
• Kantstrasse, Charlottenburg, various locations

Cathy co-founded era-defining lifestyle magazine "Style and the Family Tunes" and its website stylemag.net, and released a related fashion photo bible in 2015. She works as a creative director, and has her own charity fashion project funding eye operations. Meanwhile her French-born husband Jaybo is one of Berlin's most influential contemporary artists, represented by LA's Soze Gallery and Amsterdam's Kallenbach Gallery

Cathy Boom & Jaybo Monk, Publisher & Artist

Heartbeat of the City

Cathy might be Swiss and Jaybo French, but the creative couple couldn't be more Berlin. And it's no coincidence that their rise to prominence over the last decades matched the city's own art and fashion boom. Here, they lead us from avant-garde fashion outlets to flea markets, high-end Korean kitchens and barely legal Thai food

What keeps you in Berlin some 25 years after moving here?

Cathy: For me the city is still evolving; it's still undefined in a lot of places. That makes it an inspiration, always. And I love that Berlin is down to earth.

Jaybo: Berlin adopted me in my early 20s; gave me many opportunities to try out what I was looking for. Berlin is straightforward, for the good and the bad. And it's the town I love as soon as I am away from it.

Jaybo, as an artist, does Berlin still inspire you?

Jaybo: Every heartbeat of the city gives me inspiration. I know almost all its different shades of grey. I praise the moments of beauty beneath the rough surface. Moments without purpose, moments free of sense. The seasonal smells. The wet pavements, the morning light. Berlin has the most beautiful blue hours in winter.

Talking about the arts, which galleries should we visit?

Jaybo: *Blain Southern, Sprüth Magers, Galerie Neu, Sexauer Gallery...*

Cathy: The *Alte Nationalgalerie* and the *Gemäldegalerie*. For photography go to the *C/O Gallery* and the *Helmut Newton Museum.*

Who are the younger Berlin artists to observe at the moment?

Jaybo: Johannes Albers always finds a way to surprise me. His paintings and sculptures dance between the absurd and the deepest critique of our German society. In one exhibition he featured a very small coffin which represented our interest in government mistakes, and a giant pencil standing for the so-called importance of contracts. His humour is as sharp as a knife.

Zhivago Duncan is also interested in the decadence of society; his work reflects capitalism and consumer culture. He works with painting, sculpture, installation, kinetics—there's no material he won't use. His style is close to the US TV trash format. He mixes graffiti, comic figurines and classical expressionism. Aesthetically, he rides on the extreme. I believe he's one of the biggest to come.

Cathy, you're in fashion. Which shops and local designers are not to miss?

Cathy: *Schwarzhogerzeil* on Torstrasse offers a great selection of Dries van Noten, Isabel Marant, Cedric Charlier and Perret Schaad. Nearby, *Sabrina Dehoff* has her shop: she's an amazing jewellery designer. Further down the street on the ground floor of Soho House, *The Store* has great designers like Vetements, Marques Almeida, Balenciaga, JW Anderson and the like. The food and juices they serve are also amazing. Also in the area for men: SoTo.

For one of the best secondhand stores, head to Neukölln to *Chrome Store*. They sell high-end designer wear plus second-season collections of Berlin-based designers like Vladimir Karaleev or Hien Le. In the west, Potsdamer Strasse is worth a visit: *Acne Studios* does not especially focus on a Berlin style, but the store design is great and they offer a huge selection of their finest designs and shoes. And *Odeeh Space* in Bikini Haus—this German label has a unique style and only works with the finest materials. Their silk blouses feel like pure luxury. How they combine colour and texture in their garments is amazing!

Also check out *Esther Perbandt*, a designer devoted to the avant-garde. Let's say she's Berlin's answer to Ann Demeulemeester—lots of black and white with the finest cuts!

For easy fashion I recommend *Starstyling*. The Berlin designers

When the weather permits, Thai Park in Wilmersdorf is an explosion of authentic flavours and true Asian culture

play with spectral patterns and colourful variations, and offer the most amazing sweatshirts!

How would you spend a romantic day out in nature?

Cathy: A walk at Grunewaldsee with our dog, and a light lunch at *Chalet Suisse*. Or Glienicker Park, almost in Potsdam—the park by Glienicker Bridge where spies were exchanged in the Cold War.

Jaybo: Yes, the park there is beautiful and the trees feel ancient—a great spot to calm down from the city.

How would you spend a fun day with your daughter?

Cathy: We go to museums, photo galleries, restaurants... We like to hang out in parks like Treptower Park or Tiergarten, at flea markets like Boxhagener Platz, Arkonaplatz or Mauerpark—but only very early. Later on, Mauerpark is too full, but the karaoke in the park there is worth watching with a beer or two.

You both love good food. What are your current hot lunch spots?

Cathy: If you're a fan of Japanese, *Sasaya* offers, in my opinion, the best sushi in town. It's best to go for lunch because getting a reservation in the evening is a pain in the neck. If you get one, be on time! But it's absolutely worth it—the sushi creations and traditional dishes are a delight.

Jaybo: My favourite lunch spot is *Gobento Shiro*. The original branch is in Prenzlauer Berg but there's a newer one in Kreuzberg. Every day the chef makes a different bento box of delicious Japanese-style treats. It's small though. For pizza in the same area, *Il Casolare* is the place to go. This is old-school Kreuzberg-style, with punk-rock Italian waiters with attitude. In the summer it's nice to sit outside and look at the canal.

Cathy: You'll also find great Italian flair and food at *Salumeria Lamuri*. It has a very beautiful setting in an old butcher shop—and delicious food. For light and healthy food I prefer *The Klub Kitchen*—the sweet potato glass noodles are amazing! *DuDu* is an Asian fusion classic—it's a quick fix for lunch and never disappoints. For an authentic Thai experience on summer weekends there is a place unofficially called "Thai Park". In a public park in Wilmersdorf, lots of Thai women sit on blankets on the grass preparing and offering fresh food.

And for dining out in the evening?

Jaybo: *Dae Mon* is an amazing Korean restaurant for fine dining. And try *Kin Dee* for modern Thai cuisine with a talented young chef.

Cathy: For a trip to South Italy there's *Maselli*—amazing Italian food from Puglia, in an uncomplicated setting and cosy atmosphere and with my favourite host Angela. Another great Italian is *Briefmarken Weine*. It's in a former post office amid the crazy Socialist architecture of Karl-Marx-Allee. Good wine, solid food and a wonderful atmosphere.

Jaybo: *Lamazère* is a French bistro at its best—there's a great choice of wine and the host Regis knows how to make you happy.

Are there also cafés and bars you could recommend?

Jaybo: *Monsieur Ibrahim* at Körtestrasse has the best coffee in town. No hipsters, no scene—just regular customers.

Cathy: *Ora* is a place in an old pharmacy. The vibe is special with an old wooden environment—a little bit Viennese Kaffeehaus-style. They have great lunch, amazing cakes and excellent cocktails. *Mamecha* has a great green tea selection— I love the iced matcha latte.

Kin Dee has evolved from pop-up event to upscale Thai eatery, thanks to dishes like their whole fried fish with tamarind

Do you have a strange and secret place in town you would like to talk about?

Jaybo: No, because I need to keep my secret place secret.

Cathy: I secretly love the TV Tower—the entrance is eastern 1960s chic, with wood-panelled walls. Plus, it gives you a great idea about the concept of the city, since it is located in the exact middle point of Berlin. The view is worth a visit!

You both have a strong connection to music. What's your Berlin sound?

Cathy: 1990s hip hop is my sound of Berlin—it reminds me of the time when hip hop was underground and we started our magazine "Style and the Family Tunes". Only a few clubs in Berlin played that sound since Berlin was famous for techno. But also Peaches, Gonzales, Mocky and Jamie Lidell are my sound of Berlin. And everything dub goes

well with the city, I think.

Jaybo: Same for me—1990s hip hop, but also Einstürzende Neubauten, Caspar Brötzman, Gonzales, Whitest Boys Alive, Erland Øye.

What would make you stay another 25 more years in Berlin?

Cathy: Stay unfinished, don't sell out completely, and keep your personal style!

Jaybo: I wish Berlin a permanent month of May—stay in your teens and never grow up.

Kreuzberg & Neukölln

Over the Edge

From punk to gentrification and back again—Kreuzberg and Neukölln are fighting to maintain their scrappy reputations. So far, so good

Culture	Fermenting Creativity

When it comes to post-industrial, Berlin smacks it out of the park. And now there's a stunning addition to its transformed spaces. Berliner Kindl beer is a local symbol, and from a distance, its haunting Weimar-era brewery looks like a set from a 1920s German expressionist film. Purchased by a German-Swiss couple in 2011, it has been painstakingly converted into the *Kindl Centre for Contemporary Art*. Its spaces host large installations and exhibitions, and while the whole centre is not yet fully firing, what's open is well worth a look. Not least the café-bar in the old brewing room, with stunning copper vats and panels of buttons and dials that will regress you to infancy. The surrounding Neukölln streets are sprinkled with bars and restaurants to discover.
• Kindl Centre for Contemporary Art, Am Sudhaus 3, Neukölln, kindl-berlin.com

Kotti Soirée

Kreuzberg's Kottbusser Tor might feel dodgy at ground level, but scale the dark, concrete stairs next to the big supermarket for a surprise. At the top, on the left, *Paloma Bar* is a little club with a smart DJ lineup and the ambiance to run until sunrise. Meanwhile on the right, *Fahimi Bar* is a cocktail bar whose sleekness contrasts with the rundown view from its windows. South in Neukölln, *Sameheads* is an eclectic fashion, art and music node during the week. But when a party's on, you'll find a throbbing dancefloor and kooky lounge in its crazy, cavernous basement.
• Kreuzberg/Neukölln, various locations

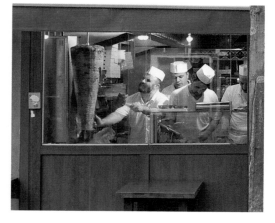

Food **Turkish Delight**

Let the smell of charcoal-roasted meat take you to a prettier place than Kottbusser Tor. The concrete development sure ain't picturesque, but, as the heart of Berlin's Turkish community, there's plenty to eat. Just off the main drag, *Doyum* (pictured) might have a kebab window, but it's a sit-down restaurant packed with Turkish diners. Try the mixed mezze, followed by the unparalleled "adana" minced-meat kebab. For the döner sandwich à la Berlin, mini-chain *Imren* has strips of beef so juicy it's like chomping on a shredded steak. The Wiener Strasse branch features wooden booths and a glitzy map of Istanbul.
• Kreuzberg, various locations

Shop **Black Crack**

Wax addicts have plenty to feast on around here. On Kreuzberg's canalside, *Hard Wax* has supplied bare-bones techno bombs and white labels for years. For Cuban throwbacks, disco edits and soulful floor fillers, *Oye* (pictured) is close by in Neukölln. West Kreuzberg newbie *Marla Records* offers a wood clad basement packed with classic hip-hop, seminal techno and the latest deep house. It also breaks the mould of moody clerks, so ask away. And at nearby *Spacehall*—where the crates run as deep as the staff's knowledge—time behaves differently. So retune your watch.
• Kreuzberg/Neukölln, various locations

Spirit of Mushin

The scruffiness of the "Kreuzkölln" borderland is belied by the fragrant notes and delicate lines at the Berlin branch of *Ryoko*. This Japanese transplant is not only a boutique and massage studio, but also hosts workshops on topics ranging from miso-making to "kintsugi", the art of broken pottery repair. You can also browse a lovingly curated assortment of paper-thin ceramics, delicate jewellery and all-natural cosmetics and fragrances made by Ryoko Hori herself. Pop in on Saturday when it's open all day, or book a massage or private shopping date online.
• Ryoko, Friedelstrasse 11, Neukölln
ryoko-berlin.com

 One for All

A serene side street detached from the traffic tumult of Kottbusser Bridge, things seem to open and close in cycles on Graefestrasse. Open since 2017, *St. Bart* has been representing the culinary confluence of German and British with seasonal dishes to share. Kreuzberg's favorite Japanese eatery, *Cocolo*, moved here from Maybachufer to serve its authentic ramen soups in a larger space. And late in the evening, it's *Minibar* (pictured) where everyone meets up for that well-mixed cocktail that defines the night.
• Kreuzberg, Graefestr., various locations

Food | **The Cool Turk**

Nevzat Ataray ran some of Istanbul's most iconic nightlife venues before he made the permanent move to Berlin. His very laid-back restaurant and bar *No Bananas* seems to somehow immortalize the cool and nonchalant essence of Istanbul's nights in the midst of Neukölln (even if the neighbors sometimes complain about the noise). Get a few things to share from the menu of classic Turkish and more experimental Mediterranean dishes and happily linger about with a few cocktails from the bar.
• No Bananas, Pannierstr. 29, Neukölln

Follow the Thread

Mitte and Charlottenburg might boast the big name stores, but for a less cookie-cutter experience shoppers should explore the city's southeastern zone. Fashion and concept shop *Voo Store* (pictured) features a world-class selection of everything from Raf Simons and Prada to Carne Bollente's embroidered sex-scene t-shirts. Grab a quality cup from in-store café *Companion Coffee* while you're there. Across the Landwehr Canal in charming Kreuzkölln, the surprisingly roomy *Chrome Store* packs racks of pre-loved designer and one-off pieces. *The Good Store* promises positivity soon—especially if that pair of vintage Dries van Noten jeans or silk Acne

jumpsuit come in your size. *Un Autre Voodoo* is the brick-and-mortar continuation of a quarterly designers' market stocking clothing, home goods and accessories. Berlin-based makers supply it with luxe lingerie, delicate jewellery and perfect commuter bags. Finally, head over to the chichi Kreuzberg mini-cosmos known as Graefekiez. There, *Süper Store* is the answer to your gift-scavenging prayers. From architectural home items to hand-embroidered Turkish linens and custom pocket knives, there's something on the shelves for every taste.

• Kreuzberg/Neukölln, various locations

Carving a Niche

Inside St. Agnes church is one of Berlin's searing-edge contemporary art spaces, König Galerie. Founder Johann has attributed his unique perspective to visual impairment as a child. His curator career began in 2003 in the German capital—a city to which he remains deeply connected today

Having converted a brutalist church into a bold art space, Johann has a deep understanding of Berlin's unusual spaces. To the sound of slapping schnitzels he points us to a gallery in the forest, bizarre nuggets of architecture, and Angela Merkel's favourite restaurant

Photo: 1) Juergen Teller. 2) Installation EUROPA, photo: BübCo Doris Kleimser

The EUROPA installation on St. Agnes Church, home to König Galerie, gives that hotly debated topic more visibility

In 1910 Karl Scheffler wrote "Berlin is condemned forever to becoming and never to being." What's your view?

In my opinion, Berlin is still one of the most amazing cities in the world. Even just a few years ago we were able to develop the brutalist church *St. Agnes* right in the heart of the city, in walking distance from Checkpoint Charlie. Though I'd been here 15 years, and my wife is from Berlin, we'd never seen that street. Berlin has things to offer I can't imagine in any other metropolis. It's a similar case with other venues, such as the art galleries Museum Frider Burder inside the former Jewish girls' school *Jüdische Mädchenschule*, and *Sammlung Boros* in an enormous wartime bunker. Countless reused sites and buildings have turned into fantastic new endeavours.

You are originally from Cologne. What brought you to Berlin?

I moved to Frankfurt when my father became dean of the art school, Städelschule. In those days I went to boarding school, and as soon as I finished I went to Berlin. That was for two reasons: firstly, I felt it was the only international city in Germany. Secondly, because I could afford it. Initially I thought of going to London, but it was too expensive. Where else could I have gone? Paris was impossible due to the language barrier. New York was not an option, because my brother had already opened a gallery there. So I decided on Berlin.

You moved here in 2003. How was Berlin in those days?

I started my gallery when still in school, by renting a space on Rosa Luxemburg Platz, opposite the

Volksbühne theatre. Today this is considered the heart of Mitte, but back then it felt like nowhereland. You couldn't find much on Rosa Luxemburg Strasse except a Hungarian travel agency, a Turkish fruit shop and a sex shop or brothel. That was it. Today it's fashion shops and all that. Rosenthaler Platz was döner central. Unfortunately, nowadays only mediocre fashion stores open there.

Which neighborhood did you choose?
First I lived in Kreuzberg, above the restaurant *Jolesch*—a fantastic neighbourhood. Conveniently, I took over the flat of my best friend Jeppe Hein, who was on a scholarship for nine months. He's the one who largely encouraged me to open the gallery, and I still represent him as an artist. I still recall the sound of the schnitzels being slapped, to make them flat, in the kitchen below. That was a familiar sound every morning, which I loved. I also remember going to different clubs in Kreuzberg. It was a really amazing time—almost 20 years ago.

Let's leave the past behind. What is the Berlin art scene like right now?
Berlin's art scene is growing and growing. But we have to be careful to make sure the artists who are not commercially successful are not pushed out of the city.

Where do you go when you are hosting a visiting artist?
When I have guests I always dream of going to *Bierpinsel*, which I never do, but would love to. Instead, I take them to a typical German place: *Altes Zollhaus*, around the corner and supposedly Angela Merkel's favourite restaurant. It is next to the Landwehr Canal. Then I take them to somewhere like *Themroc, Bar3, Chez Michel* or *Richard*, and if they are

from abroad, to Sammlung Boros. I also show them the usual museums.

So what are the usual museums?
A must-see is always *Akademie der Künste*, designed by Werner Düttmann—the same architect who designed St. Agnes. A legend of post-war Berlin architecture. I also like the off-the-beaten-track museums like *Haus am Waldsee*. In my opinion *Berlinische Galerie* has the best contemporary programme. They do the most interesting combination of photography and architecture.

Where do you take your children to appreciate art?
I try not to push too much, because I come from an art background myself. You just live through it and I think art is not so much for kids. Though my children did appreciate Tomás Saraceno at *Hamburger Bahnhof*—actually more than I did. Having said that, he's a great friend and fantastic artist. They also enjoyed Otto Piene at the Neue Nationalgalerie—though that museum is closed for renovation now. And at Haus am Waldsee one of their favourites is the ongoing mini-golf.

If St. Agnes church—which houses your gallery—were to be painted, which artist would you choose?
The building has no real colour because it follows brutalist architectural rules—it's the material's own brown-grey colour. But if we painted it, I would definitely choose Katharina Grosse. I'd get it spray-painted in all possible colours of brightness.

And if you could replicate your gallery project in another building?
My favourite building is Ludwig Leo's *Versuchsanstalt für Wasserbau*

Former rail station Hamburger Bahnhof has hosted some epic art, like this work by Isa Genzken and Wolfgang Tillmans

und Schiffbau in Berlin. That would be an interesting one.

How would you spend a day off?
That's simple. I'd head to Zehlendorf, further south-west, and take a walk with my friend Jeppe Hein around the lake Krumme Lanke. Afterwards I'd have lunch at *Café Einstein Stammhaus*.

Where else do you like to eat out?
There is a brunch place called *Brachvogel*, close to the Landwehr Canal and St. Agnes, where you can have fantastic brunch and play minigolf on Sundays. For lunch I like the St. Agnes cafeteria

or *Ishin*. For dinner, the usual suspects: *Grill Royal* and *Yarok*— an amazing Syrian deli on Torstrasse—that is in fact my favourite.

Is something missing in Berlin?
Initially, I wanted to say more wealth. But this has changed in the last years. I think what is quintessentially missing is better dressed people. I really appreciate it in Paris or New York, to see how people look after themselves.

Innocence and Wonder

Tobias Remberg

Though my parents hadn't even met in 1963 when John F. Kennedy made his legendary "Ich bin ein Berliner" speech, that sentiment is the core of my existence. Save for a misguided three-year stint, I've lived in Berlin my entire life. For better or worse—it defines and confines me.

Photo: Courtesy of Tresor Berlin

Over the years I've fallen in love with the world's great cities. Tokyo with its bright-light excitement granted me no sleep at all. New York put an almost mystical spell upon me. And I could see myself Ubering through London for weeks. But would I want to live in these towns? The answer is an emphatic "No way, JFK!"

My city and I have been through too much together. I couldn't bear to miss what's next. Berlin has had its share of different incarnations. And all of them have been exciting, in their own quirky ways.

I was born into East Berlin, capital of the German Democratic Republic, and spent some of the late 1970s and the 1980s dealing with it. This was a town divided by an actual wall from its western part—the western part jokingly referred to as "the island in the Red Sea". But we were also divided, by an invisible wall, from the rest of East Germany. Compared to that socialist hinterland, life in East Berlin was actually pretty decent. The sick and twisted regime always tried to save face through its capital. We were a piece of Communist window-dressing, something which made life for us a little easier on the eye—and on the stomach, for that matter—than in the rest of the country. For instance, everything that was to be imported into our country made it first to Berlin and its population. Only a fraction ever made it out. Maybe they were little, even silly, things. But who would want to live without bananas in their lives? And due to the proximity of West Berlin, Western TV and radio was a huge part of our educational and entertainment diet.

It was the little things that kept us in line, because it wasn't really fun to pass the Berlin Wall in those days without getting angry about being a Cold War hostage forbidden from walking a hundred metres to the left or right. As far as we knew back then, that wall would be there forever. It was messed up. I remember one day little Tobi broke with the system. On a beach in Romania a friendly granny gave me a Mickey Mouse book. On the return flight home it was confiscated by GDR customs, as it was deemed capitalist propaganda. I was lucky that my parents didn't ever buy into the fairytales. When we were within our own four walls, there was no sugar-coating—we ridiculed everything that came out of the regime's many mouths. And when we left home, my parents to work and me to school, we put on a mask and played along, in the least enthusiastic fashion possible. To say that was an interesting way to live is putting it mildly. It was more of a schizophrenic, Kafkaesque experience. As the 1980s slowly rolled by, the East German economy grew ever more stagnant, and the communist regimes around us dropped like flies. Meanwhile at school, the teachers still told us we were the tenth strongest industrial nation in the world. Comedy gold!

In turn the Iron Curtain became less impermeable—the masses had to be appeased somehow. On a few occasions my parents were allowed to visit relatives in West Germany for special occasions like the 60th birthday of a second cousin or something. There was a complicated law about it—another twisted piece in the narrative of control. Of course spouses were never allowed to travel together, let alone take their kids, because then they'd have had no reason to ever come back and play their crucial part in holding the Communist dream afloat. I envied my parents these trips. All those shiny things they brought back weren't all that satisfying given their travel tales were only fuelling my ever-growing anger over my confinement.

But the government had something else in stock to appease kids like me. In March 1988 they let a spaceship land in Berlin. With only a few days' notice it was announced that Depeche Mode were to play a gig in East Berlin. We're talking about by far the most beloved band among East German teenagers, so that was a huge deal. The only problem? You couldn't buy one of the 6,000 tickets. They handed out two tickets to every Berlin class from 9th to 12th grade. And those tickets only went to kids who played a vital part in the Communist youth organisation FDJ, which was organising the gig. I was lucky enough to persuade our class's FDJ leader to sell me his ticket for almost nothing. Thankfully he was more into trains. At the concert hall, the scene was indescribable. It felt like every East German teenager had showed up—and only a fraction had a ticket. Absurd amounts of money—and motorbikes—were exchanged for these cherished pieces of paper. It was mayhem, and for a long few minutes I thought I'd be trampled to death before I reached the doors. The gig itself was epic. It was our Beatles at Shea Stadium moment—with less screaming and better sound. Later that summer my parents and I and another 160,000 people went to see Bruce Springsteen. That time it was our Woodstock, sans the LSD of course. The Wall was cracking. And it would never recover.

I was already asleep when my father woke me up on November 9th, 1989 and asked me if I fancied a stroll along Kurfürstendamm. "Hell yes," I said. With my uncle and cousin we crossed the border at Chausseestrasse at midnight, joy-jumping through the delirious crowd. I couldn't believe my luck. I was 17, and from one second to another, the WHOLE world was mine. Even if that—for now—just meant a walk on Kurfürstendamm, bed at four, and back to school a few hours later.

The next few months were a blur. East Berlin still looked the same, but it clearly wasn't. The rapid decay of every authority that had kept the people in check created an "anything goes"–environment you had to live through to completely grasp. My friends and I spent every second we could mapping out the unknown—crossing the checkpoints into West Berlin. Shopping and cinemas in Charlottenburg and Schöneberg, football games at Olympiastadion and the furious indie melting pot of Kreuzberg. En route we debunked a few of our own myths about the shiny West, which we'd romanticised during our grey confinement. West Berlin wasn't so different from our part after all. The same boring and dreary sectors, the same disturbingly depressing tower blocks in the suburbs... In fact, the social tensions were far more intense than what we were accustomed to. Life in the East might have been boring but it was always safe and without real economic hardship.

And then in 1990 a funny thing started to happen. Kids from West Berlin, whom we'd quickly learned weren't really different from us, started to take on the East, with the same wide-eyed excitement we'd had a couple of months before. They'd also been confined for all these years and could now explore the East and meet new people. After a year and a half I had as many "Westfriends" as "Eastfriends". We just merged and never looked back—and quickly even stopped thinking in those terms.

I was still in school, 11th and 12th grade, and life was carefree. Even the teachers didn't care at that point—it had been too much change in too little time for them. It wasn't like we didn't learn anything, but there was little to no pressure, and there was also weed. I was basically lost to the Stone Roses, Happy Mondays, "Twin Peaks" and techno. As far as I was concerned it couldn't get better. We'd spend weekends at Tresor or Planet, clubs so damn exciting that even today's Berghain pales in comparison.

We couldn't care less about politics in those days. While Reunification came with a lot of hardship, injustices and broken promises for many, we were just out partying. That might seem superficial, but at least we were reunited and didn't have to bicker with each other. I was sponging it all up. Imagine, only three years before, the extent of my interaction with different nationalities peaked at kissing a Polish girl once. Now I was cuddling with big black dudes from New York City, raiding the penny jar to buy a kebab with my Iranian friend, sitting backstage at a club listening to the tales of Neil Tennant or Carl Cox, or enjoying Monday sushi and videos with a French-English Catholic girl. We loved and learned from each other; to this day these friends remain the backbone of my social circle. For a huge chunk of the 1990s the lack of bureaucracy and rules made Berlin a universe of endless possibilities. Not just for me, but for the city itself, this was the age of innocence and wonder.

Inevitably, the tide began to turn. When the office staff at the club E-Werk were held robbed at gunpoint while everybody else continued to enjoy the party downstairs—the innocence had faded. Well, the city had to grow up sometime. And we had to grow up with it. Yet despite gentrification and the repression of subcultures, Berlin remains dynamic, now fuelled by the influx of money, know-how and foreigners. The Berlin Promise keeps them coming in as the city enters yet another incarnation. And whatever happens, I'll be here to see what's next.

Tobias Remberg is a poet and a scholar, football writer and Britpop fanatic. Born and raised in East Berlin, you can still find him roaming the streets of the city with a pencil behind his ear and a wild innocence in his eyes

04

Nihad Tule
Sebastian Bayne

Mo
House of Waxx

Globus

Juniper
Jason Fellows
SARJ

22

Mile Music/JP

Soul People Music, UQ/US

Ostgut Ton, Madhouse/UK

Elephant Moon/Berlin

Tresor Records, Deeply Rooted/Paris

Vidab/Berlin

Tresor.Berlin

06

Brown Rice/Berlin

Macro/Berlin

TLFT, Sneaky Pete s/Edinburgh

Dimitri is an undisputable
Berlin legend—a prime mover
who made the city what it is
today. After the Wall came
down he founded seminal club
Tresor, and later, the Atonal
music festival. Nowadays he
works with creative projects
of all stripes, such as turning
industrial ruins into spaces
thriving with culture and life

Dimitri Hegemann, Club Owner

Let Them Play

Berlin past, present and future is represented in the person of Dimitri,
who still retains a sense of magical wonder regarding the city.
He reveals which club gets closest to that 1990s feeling, shares some
spots to head to on two wheels, and recounts a few stories from
those good and messy old days

You arrived in Berlin in 1978—what were your first impressions?

Very curious; very excited. I had left my town because the older people didn't let us play. My parents had come from WWII; while I was very inspired by all the images of Woodstock. So we wanted to set up a community centre and make music together and be hippies. But all these authority figures like teachers, parents, police, the ghosts of the past, didn't want us to have fun. So I left to Berlin and found people with similar stories. We'd been kicked out, in a way. We came into a Berlin that was a big city, but felt small. I discovered the city over two, three years. I didn't know many people but I managed to get my culture fix—I was studying Musicology at the time and our professors would talk about punk and new wave. That was something happening here in real time. I remember The Cure's first show here, Joy Division, The Police... I saw things that I haven't seen since. I think people looked more eccentric then than now. Maybe I was blinded by the light, but there was definitely something I'd never seen.

You consider yourself a "space pioneer"—how have these spaces shaped Berlin?

Back then, you had these giant gaps in the city, from the bombings and the clearings. When the Wall came down it was like a giant historic gift. In West Berlin, you had all these people with great ideas who were missing space. So when the Wall came down everyone flooded the East and these subcultures finally matured and found a space to develop. Anyone who wanted to start a gallery or a club could find a space. Anything you wanted to do, you could do.

Is that how Tresor started?

We were already busy with music projects—a small record company, importing music from Detroit. When we came across this vault, we were blown away. I was making records but we needed a stage to play. That was the idea behind starting a club—setting our own stage. That's how Tresor started.

How were those beginnings?

Thanks to reunification, lots of kids came from both East and West. First, there was fresh music and secondly, both sides liked it. This music from Detroit arrived in Berlin and just took off; it came at exactly the right moment. But the third factor, and this is vital, is we had no curfew. Imagine, the euphoria about reunification was huge, and everyone had all this freedom to celebrate it. When we rented this place, we'd sign a lease for two months and renew it again and again. It was crazy. This was the beginning of it all. I was infected. Everybody was. There was this atmosphere—it was history and we were a part of it. I wasn't aware of it at the time, but looking back you could say I was a part of it.

Are there any places in Berlin now that remind you of that era?

I was recently in a place that reminded me of it—a friend, Wax Treatment, was playing at *Griessmühle* down in Neukölln. I walked in and it was dark and the sound system was nice, and it reminded me of the first days, everything improvised and very rough. Now we have all these controls, and it's not that easy to survive anymore.

You seem forward-facing—how would you respond to people who grumble about Berlin not being cool anymore?

If you're here for two days, you

Loved by the locals, Renger-Patzsch is a good place to rub elbows with Berlin's old guard over the quality "flammkuchen"

Winterfeldmarkt
Schöneberg

Markthalle Neun
Kreuzberg

Renger-Patzsch
Schöneberg

Café Einstein
Stammhaus
Schöneberg

FSK
Kreuzberg

Yorck Kino
Kreuzberg

Mr. Minsch
Kreuzberg

might not find time to experience it. But if you've got the chance, stay longer. Grab a bike, explore the city, museums, open spaces. There's so much going on creatively. I can promise if you're here long enough you'll find at least one person you like, who shares your ideas. It's these people who make the city what it is. When I go to other cities and see how much they rush, I realise Berlin is paradise. My main concern, frankly, is that the secret will get out and too many people will come! It's very tolerant here.

And where do you go when you grab your bike?

I like markets—like the *Winter-feldmarkt*, or Thursdays and Saturdays at *Markthalle Neun*. My main areas are Kreuzberg and Schöneberg.

What about Schöneberg? Any favourite haunts?

I love *Renger-Patzsch*, they do wonderful flammkuchen. I still go to places like Café M, which used to be called Café Mitropa. That was the name of the East German catering company on the trains running through the Iron Curtain. They'd serve you Mitropa mugs and you'd steal them and bring them back to West Berlin. I also really like *Café Einstein Stammhaus* on Kurfurstenstrasse.

Anything else you like in the city?

I love movie theatres. Everyone speaks English now so the movies are in English. I like *FSK* for the weirder movies. I love the Yorck cinema chain. Close to *Yorck Kino* there's a place called *Mr. Minsch*. It's a shop run by a group of women who bake cakes all day.

Borchardt's
Mitte

Grill Royal
Mitte

Ora
Kreuzberg

And where do you take guests to eat when you want to impress?

If you've managed to book in advance, *Borchardt's* or *Grill Royal*. But if it's not such a fancy night, I love the old pharmacy restaurant, *Ora*. Also, pretty much anything on Görlitzer Strasse or Wiener Strasse is a safe bet for eating. Same goes for Kastanienallee. I actually could spend my life in a very small circle, like back in my village. In West Berlin I lived on Köpenicker Strasse, when I had my gallery the Fischbüro. And now I'm here, still on the same street. The wall came down and my life still stayed on Köpenicker.

The Fischbüro is an old-school Berlin legend—what went on there?

It was a place for coming together. We'd introduce someone, like Anna. We'd say "It's her first time here and she wants to tell you about her clothes." So maybe she'd give a presentation and get shyly up on stage and whisper "I got this jacket for one euro" and everybody would yell and cheer her on, through her presentation for her entire outfit. Then the next person, Johann, would read us "two telephone numbers!" And everyone would go crazy as he slowly read his best friend's ex-girlfriend's phone number aloud. He'd come back for an encore with nothing less than a telephone number from a friend in Amsterdam. A Dutch number! People would cheer and laugh. It was a close-knit group, very warm and welcoming. It was a new kind of intensity, because where before it was just stand in line, pay your ten bucks to watch a show and go home, here I had discovered the power of conversation. The idea was always to have fun. It was a tiny, welcoming space. People loved it; they would say "you saved my life, now I'm someone". After reading

phone numbers people would work up the nerve to bring in their poetry. Sometimes it was horrible but everyone supported them.

Does this tie in with your current social project, The Happy Locals?

It comes from my own experience in my village. I was forced out and came to Berlin to create spaces of my own. When these kids get older in their villages and towns, they don't feel identified with the spaces provided for them. Young people are hungry for culture and if you don't feed them what they need, they'll go elsewhere to satisfy that need. What stays behind are more mainstream tastes, people who make it easier for right-wing ideas to take hold. So you have to create relevant, independent spaces for people to feel fulfilled. Perhaps insert a mentor figure, someone who encourages young people to do things the right way—to ask for a permit to do a graffiti mural, to discourage dealing drugs, or wasting time. To lobby for the resources needed to fulfil these interests and cultural needs. The Happy Locals is a kind of blueprint for the creation of these spaces and programmes to keep people happy without leaving their towns.

What can you tell us about Berlin's nightlife these days?

Berlin is very lucky that we have no curfew and a healthy night time economy. We get 32 million hotel stays a year, not counting Airbnb. These people come and spend about 250 euros a day, and many come because of our nightlife. When the Wall fell, this underground movement became strong—these days they call it creative industries—and evolved into one of the city's strongest economic forces. All these open spaces, the freedom to create and

Nightclub and former grain mill Griessmühle is a haven for house, techno and disco. A quintessential Berlin experience

a lack of curfew helped create this Berlin. This is a formula I'm trying to help the mayor of Detroit understand. They need more people—young, intelligent people interested in culture, to create a tolerant environment. Learning from Berlin, I'd say open up their night and let the young people play. If Detroit cancelled its curfew, it could support a healthy club culture; you'd have agencies, industries popping up. You have a city with an incredible music history and all this space—they just need to go in the right direction.

And what's your wish for Berlin?
    I'd love for Berlin to stay just the way it is. I'd like for people to understand, especially the authorities, that Berlin needs this freedom for the arts. The artistic freedom

needs to remain. The city will need to continue supporting subcultures, find a middle ground between artistic development and commercial. On June 20, 1949 Berlin cancelled its curfew and nothing was ever the same for us. I hope things stay that way, because so many things depend on it. My dream is to put together a team of Happy Locals to help revitalise other cities and towns.

Bridging the Border

A showcase by Ilse Ruppert

The lens that truly captured 1980s Berlin was wielded by Ilse Ruppert, who also made her name by portraying punk and New Wave scenes in New York City, London, Paris and Hamburg. This selection from the two halves of the divided capital presents contrasts and parallels: decadence, camaraderie, poignancy and hope

A former wrestler from Dresden takes a break
from working on a Prenzlauer Berg street
—East Berlin, 1982

"Colonel" looks out over Christinenstrasse
—East Berlin, 1982

"While living in Hamburg in the 1980s, I'd often get calls from record companies when they had bands in town. One night I got a couple of calls from Iggy Pop. "Please, angel—get me some coke", or "You bitch! Where is the stuff?" The next day I came into the office and he just sat there, staring at me. "No coke?" Pretty funny! I liked him anyway"
—Ilse Ruppert

Wolfgang Müller, founder of performance art and music group Die Tödliche Doris, sits across from burlesque dancer Valerie Caris Ruhnke (middle) and artist Reinhardt Wilhelmi (right) —West Berlin, 1984

Billy Wagner, Restaurateur & Sommelier
In Vino Veritas

A frequent "Sommelier of the Year", Billy has dealt the grape in some of Germany's top restaurants. He remains sommelier and host at Berlin's Weinbar Rutz, as well as being co-founder of the one-Michelin-star restaurant Nobelhart & Schmutzig, a big influence in the capital's culinary canon

Billy is surfing the wave of New Berlin Cuisine—but he's still as passionate about casual bites as high-end dishes. Handmade marzipan, authentic ramen, Texan BBQ and more all illustrate the diversity of Berlin's dining scene—and he even stops off for dawn at Berghain

You've worked across Germany. What drew you to Berlin in 2008?

A job offer. I had the choice between the acclaimed restaurant Sansibar on the North Sea island of Sylt or in Berlin's famous *Weinbar Rutz*. Not much to consider—Berlin beats Sylt hands down.

The Berlin dining scene has transformed over the last decade. Why?

It has become really diverse here. That's true not only for the top restaurants, but the whole scene: from simple BBQ stands to a funky dim sum shop or a super Thai. On the level of starred restaurants, the variety is greater than ever before. Berlin has simply profited from the influx of people from all over the world and the experience they bring to the city.

Which places best showcase this diversity?

Markthalle Neun certainly has a diverse selection of food stalls—on Friday or Saturday from noon on, get a bite from Anna at Big Stuff BBQ, washed down with a "Thirsty Lady" from the Heidenpeters brewery. Aperitivo culture, though big in Paris or Rome nowadays, is still not too strong in Berlin. Also one of my favourite wine bars is *Briefmarken Weine* on Karl-Marx-Allee—with some of the best pasta north of the Alps. And for Japanese ramen, try *Takumi Nine* for great noodle soup in a classic setting.

What about the tea-and-coffee scene?

There are a lot of people who are total nerds when it comes to coffee machines, beans and preparation. Take the *Oslo Kaffebar*. It's located behind an unassuming façade, there are simple wooden tables, you can also buy records—but this where some of the best coffee in the city is served. Otherwise, you could also visit *Five Elephant* or *The Barn*

Roastery. Something else which is very exciting and has barely been covered is the subject of tea. *Paper & Tea* is the place to find tea-freaks creating absolutely inventive blends and a compelling new tea culture.

What about in the realm of dessert?

Coda is a "dessert bar" in Kreuzkölln, the borderland between Kreuzberg and Neukölln. Rene Frank is a former three-star patissier; they combine great cocktails there with super fine, elegant desserts.

Talking about innovation in gastronomy —where are the places to go?

Horváth on Paul-Lincke-Ufer. In terms of the food it's one of the most exciting restaurants in the city. Even though it's not vegetarian, there's a strong focus on locally grown, traditional varieties of vegetables. There's a clear awareness of how to use and prepare food. The chefs work with charcoal or smoking to highlight the taste of the product—but without fanfare. Sebastian Frank is, for me, one of the most innovative chefs in the city. I also recommend Restaurant *Einsunternull*. The chef Andreas Rieger presents a very exciting local cuisine. The affordable lunch menu on Tuesday to Saturday is a must— three courses of very high quality for just 29 euros. Another interesting spot is *Herz und Niere*—the name translates as "heart and kidney" and it's a nose-to-tail concept with locally sourced ingredients. Look out for the upcoming restaurant Ernst, by my former colleague Christoph Geyler. When it opens that will be my pick for Berlin's first three-star kitchen.

What can we expect at your one-star restaurant Nobelhart & Schmutzig?

A warm and honest cuisine— high-end, proudly local food—and

Herz und Niere is steadfast in its "nose-to-tail" philosophy, offering guests the chance to try cuisine beyond tenderloin filet

an enjoyable experience, all in a unpolished setting. You'll be sitting around the kitchen. We keep close ties to local producers.

Which bars do you find interesting?
There is *Becketts Kopf, Buck & Breck, Immertreu, Tier* and *Bar Lebensstern* above Café Einstein Stammhaus on Kurfürstenstrasse. These are all locations that stand for a unique style of bar culture.

Let's talk about wine. Which type would you associate most with the city?
Riesling is like Berlin. It's the most German of all varieties of grapes, and also the most diverse.

What's typical Berlin food and where can we find it?
I recommend the "soljanka"—a thick, spicy soup—at *Die Berliner Republik*. The best currywurst is at

Witty's, close to KaDeWe department store. To find the best local sausages and cheese, order the "Brandenburger Teller" at *Weinstein.* And I have to say that our blood sausage at Weinbar Rutz is legendary.

What culinary products would make a nice souvenir from the city?
A craft beer from a young brewery couldn't go wrong, especially as Berlin was famous for its brewing tradition in the old days. Or go to *Preussische Spirituosen Manufaktur* for hand-crafted liqueurs essential to the local bar culture. These include special varieties such as galangal or ginger liqueur, all free of additives, which can also be enjoyed straight. Another original Berlin choice is *Wald Königsberger Marzipan.* They've hand-made marzipan for four generations. You can always find a small, sweet souvenir there.

Former stamp shop Briefmarken's stationery has been replaced by choice wines and homemade pasta

What else should not be missed on a weekend in Berlin?

A three-hour boat trip on the Spree river and the Landwehr Kanal is a must. It might sound touristy, but it's how to see Berlin at its best and appreciate how incredibly beautiful and green it is. Another key moment is standing in the Panorama Bar of superclub *Berghain* after a good breakfast on Sunday. When there's a great track playing and the blinds open up—this is typical of Berlin. Then, to relax on Sunday evening, visit *Fontane Therme*—a beautiful spa with perfect views onto the lake.

Let's flash forward to Berlin, 2025. What will the scene be like?

Most chefs will eliminate the unnecessary and emphasise proximity with the guest. Berlin will benefit from an even larger stream of worldwide influences. The region around Berlin will be in full bloom 35 years after the fall of the Wall, and city people will rekindle their relationship with nature in search of tranquility. In the highly technological world of the future this aspect will be more essential.

Tiergarten & Schöneberg

Landing Strip

Potsdamer Strasse was a key artery 100 years ago—recipient of the city's first traffic light. But after the Wall came up, it was more about red lights. Now, the area is back: packed with great food and top art

| Culture | Pick up the Pieces |

No other street in the city has a higher density of galleries. Around and on Potsdamer Strasse over 50 different spaces cater to varoius tastes and needs—from big international flagships like *Blain Southern* to traditional German names like *Aurel Scheibler*, originally founded in 1990s Cologne. Meanwhile, publishing company *Helga Maria Klosterfelde* is now run by her son Alfons. The institution is mostly famous for publishing heavy hitters like Rosemarie Trockel or Mat Mullican, while hosting shows for young talents like Cécile B. Evans and Yuri Pattison. Based in the yard where the "Tagesspiegel" newspaper used to be,

Galerie Thomas Fischer focusses on young contemporary art, exploring the intersection between tradition and multimedia. *Société*'s roster of young artists like Bunny Smith and Trisha Baga makes it worth finding the gallery, tucked away as it is down a backstreet. And *Circle Culture Gallery*— a major player dedicated to creators with a background in urban art—moved from Mitte to the burgeoning art strip a few years back, rubberstamping the new centre of Berlin's art market. Don't be surprised if more spaces pop up before too long.

• Tiergarten, various locations

Fresh and Local

Tasty little *Winterfeldmarkt* is balanced midpoint between Berlin's fancy West and grungy East. Likewise, it manages to combine locally sourced produce with hearty German comfort food. Short-term visitors will have less use for the farm-fresh groceries, but there are plenty of options for on-the-go chow. Look out for lip-smacking grilled fish-in-a-bun from Steckerlfisch, and Bauer Lindner's sausages, produced sustainably at a nearby ranch. The market is only open Wednesday and Saturday, but the square's cafés are just as charming during the rest of the week.

• Winterfeldmarkt, Winterfeldplatz, Schöneberg

Shop | Hopelessly Devoted

This is no art installation, despite the area's concentration of small galleries. Far from satirising religion, *Ave Maria* celebrates it: this is an oasis of Catholicism in the heart of cynical Berlin. In its bewildering interior find figurines ranging from pocket-sized to gigantic, plus rosaries, charms, amulets, a font of holy water and plenty more to cause wonder, regardless of your faith. Presided over by irrepressible Neapolitan Rachele Cutulo, the shop is a meeting point for immigrant communities, local pimps, wayward clubbers, and incense addicts seeking a transportative scent from over 40 varieties.

• Ave Maria, Lützowstrasee 23, Tiergarten

Shop | Conceptualism

Berlin's concept-store king is pushing the retail envelope with two shops on this street. *Andreas Murkudis 81* is a 1,000 square-metre former newspaper building, redone in post-industrial chic and stocked with curated clothes, creams and design items. His second store at number *77* adds furnishing and interior-design elements to the mix. The street's creative-retail climate is crowned by Fiona Bennett's *Hut-Palast*—an airy light-filled space colourfully piled with hats. The Brighton-born milliner was taught by Vivienne Westwood. Her creations might have graced the wide world— but her creative headspace is here.

• Tiergarten, various locations

Food | Spices of Life

The strip between Schöneberger Ufer and Winterfeldplatz is no longer than two kilometres but the culinary diversity couldn't stretch wider. All the classic Berlin goodies are here, from a fresh falafel at *Habibi* and solid Turkish BBQ at *Pascha Grill*, to decent Thai curry at *Samran*. But the area also has specific offers hard to find elsewhere. *Ixthys* is a small and simple Korean restaurant where no beer is served and the walls are surreally decorated with Bible verses. A few steps east, *Da Jia Le* is the only spot in town serving Dongbei cuisine from northeastern China. And it's phenomenal. Long-standing Japanese fast-food joint *Tori-Katsu* is a fine place for the eponymous breaded cutlet, a Japanese classic originally inspired by the schnitzel but modified in the East. Meanwhile next door, *Nafis* is dedicated to Persian cuisine—the staff are super friendly and the dishes reliably authentic. Try traditional desserts like the saffron rice pudding. Mixed platters with Ethiopian specialities are the order at *Bejte Ethiopia* (pictured)—on the weekends it can get foggy when the team roasts coffee in the basement. Can't decide? *Maiden Mother & Crone* could help, with daily lunch specials from around the world—the Moroccan tajines are fingerlicking.

• Schöneberg & Tiergarten, various locations

Night **Sophisticated Mix**

Potsdamer Strasse was a streak of urban desert in 2001 when Stefan Weber and friends opened *Victoria Bar*. He placed his own eclectic art collection on the walls, and devised a drinks list so refined and well-executed Gault Millaut named him best barkeeper of that year. In fact, he and his co-founders know their drinks so well, they literally wrote the book on it. That's "The School of Sophisticated Drinking", now available in English translation. Clearly there's a lot to learn—but hitting the bar is a good place to start.
• Victoria Bar, Potsdamer Strasse 102, Tiergarten, victoriabar.de

Food **From Breakfast to Lunch**

It was the love between a dog named Rocket and a cat named Basil that inspired the name of this cafe. Founded by sisters Sophie and Xenia, two German Iranians who grew up in Australia, *Rocket & Basil* reflects the culinary traditions of their unique mixed heritage. Seasonal dishes bring together unexpected flavours and really showcase the sisters' love for food, which spurred more than fifteen years of food industry experience. Order a salad, snack, pastry or one of the signature stews.
• Rocket & Basil, Lützowstraße 22, Tiergarten rocketandbasil.com

Night **Buddy Pad**

When you're ready to crash down from orbit onto the rocky surface of the moon, a Berliner institution awaits in the form of *Kumpelnest 3000*. It was opened by local hero Mark Ernestus in 1987 as an art project, and quickly became a vital loop in Berlin's nocturnal rollercoaster. Which other nightspots can boast both a past Karl Lagerfeld photoshoot with Claudia Schiffer, and regular parties for the deaf? This free-entry, 24-hour bar-club sucks in all colourful night travellers. But beware—some never leave.
• Kumpelnest 3000, Lützowstr. 23, Tiergarten, kumpelnest3000.com

Tiergarten & Schöneberg

Anita Tillmann, Fashion Entrepreneur
Mode Selector

After picking up the thread with fashion brands like Joop! and Kathleen Madden, Anita exploded in 2003 with her international fashion show Premium. Soon after, she was expanding Berlin's scene with trailblazing fairs like Seek, Panorama, Bright, Show&Order, and the innovation-focussed #Fashiontech

She might hail originally from Düsseldorf, but Anita is an organic part of today's Berlin. She shares killer spots for seasoned visitors, kitchens that offer a smart business lunch, and some of the sharpest young designers on the fizzing local fashion scene

Your fashion trade shows attract a global audience. Why is Berlin special for them?

Berlin is unique when it comes to creative power. There is no other city in Europe with such a throng of creative, young people from all around the world. This is where fashion, art, music, design and innovation collide and generate a strong, creative energy. Berlin has changed a lot in just ten years. The former rave capital of the 1990s is now a relevant fashion metropolis with an unbelievably strong economic influence.

Speaking about contemporary fashion and design, what does Berlin offer?

Berlin offers plenty of new store concepts. Our Berlin-based buyers and the city's fashion community represent a tribe, leading a movement and broadcasting their lifestyle through social media and influencing like-minded people all over the world. In the whole of Europe, Berlin is the one spot where new stores are opened and new concepts are introduced first. On top of that, Berlin is the home of elevated streetwear, young talent as well as established designers. Berlin offers a street scene, inspiring new spots that pop up at every corner, as well as interesting influencers.

Could you name five talents to watch in these areas?

Nobi Talai, William Fan, Marina Hoermanseder, Michael Sontag and Tim Labenda, but also a brand like 032c. They have been recognised through their beautiful designs but also through their professionalism and business sense—essential assets when it comes to creating a brand. The designer Nobi Talai was born in Tehran and is embracing her

nomadic heritage through all her collections. Her signature designs show her love for textiles and forms. William Fan has become one of Berlin's most promising designers. His brand has overcome boundaries when it comes to sex, age or season. Marina Hoermanseder's trademarks are leather straps and lacquer outfits. With these, she has managed to bridge artistic creations and commercial collections, staying true to herself. Michael Sontag creates casual collections with a very elegant look, using only the most luxurious textiles like silk, cashmere or wool, and has stayed true to himself from his first collection onwards. Although Tim Labenda started his career as a menswear designer, he was discovered by Christiane Arp with his first womenswear collection and has established himself as one of the most promising German designers, making every collection an experience. And 032c is a new Berlin-based shirt brand, which is already being hyped internationally as the new big thing.

Could you describe the typical Berlin fashionista uniform?

There is no uniform in Berlin and that's exactly what makes it inspiring and vibrant. What you see everywhere, though, are sneakers and a street style that everyone interprets in their own unique way. People in this city wear and mix designer clothes, and it always looks effortless and easy.

What is your preferred location for business lunches and dinners these days?

For business lunches we often go to *Café Einstein*, a smart spot on Unter den Linden, *Cecconi's*, the Italian restaurant at Soho House, *Borchardt's* for fancy, traditional German fare downtown or *Ishin* for sushi. For dinner I prefer *Grill Royal*, *Crackers* and *Golden Phoenix* at the Provocateur Hotel for French-Chinese fusion by Mr. Duc Ngo—or the exclusive Japanese restaurant *893 Ryotei*, which is always packed with an international, interesting crowd.

If you have friends from abroad visiting—and it's not their first time—where would you take them?
That's the best situation. We organise private, guided tours through Berlin's gallery scene, which is always impressive. In summertime we rent a boat and discover Berlin's lake and nature diversity. Naturally we tour the shops, starting in famous department store *KaDeWe* and contemporary shopping centre *Bikini Berlin*, traversing the city centre with all the stores along Torstrasse, and ending up in Kreuzberg at *Voo Store*. Berlin's food scene embraces modern and creative food ideas. Concepts like street-food market *Markthalle Neun*, raw food restaurant *Daluma*, one-star "food bar" *Nobelhart & Schmutzig*, upmarket German kitchen *PeterPaul*, and casual fine dining restaurant *Lode & Stijn*, are popping up constantly. There's no chance to keep up! I always take my guests to the Soho House membership club.

How do you unwind when you're not working?
The ride through the city around the chancellery to the Tiergarten park is really nice and worth seeing. Also, the area around the Bodemuseum is beautiful and I like sitting by the the Spree River, which flows through the whole city.

You also have two kids—how to you enjoy the city with them?
Berlin is child-friendly and all kids are outdoor kids. There are so many different and really nice playgrounds, even in the Tiergarten. There are various jump houses, climbing centres and interesting museums like the *Naturkundemuseum*. The cultural kids' programme is huge—from museums to small and big theatres.

What are three things you don't like about the city?
It's dirty, and the green areas—which are really a public luxury from my perspective—are not cultivated. It's a shame. Also I don't like it when people from Berlin always complain about their own city without giving anything back to it. The people who travel know how amazing Berlin is from many different points of view.

And the three things you miss when you're away?
I miss the openness, easiness and effortlessness of Berlin. And, after all these years, I can say I love this city and it has been a love affair from day one.

Do you have a future vision for Berlin? How would you like the city to be in 2022?
Berlin represents democracy, freedom, multiculturalism and human rights like no other city. Germany stands for innovation and economic strength. This has to be strengthened and protected. I am very positive that Berlin will be the beacon of a free and better life all over the world. I personally would appreciate better schools, clean streets and cultivated park areas.

The entrance hall to Grill Royal is just as elegant as the restaurant itself. It's the choice cuts of meat that do the talking here

Mode Selector

Fundgrube

Gorilla Feminism

This shirt's design reportedly led the trainers of Koko the gorilla to discover she reads handwriting as well as printed words. Created by Berlin-based female collective Kirr.
• Kirr sweatshirt, keepitreallyreal.com

Pad it Out

The mark of a certified techno institution—bring a couple of these home to look like an instant clubbing connoisseur. Now all you need are the turntables.
• Hardwax slipmats, hardwax.com

Fine China

A Berlin classic gets the fancy treatment. These china "trays" are made for your finest sausage with spiced ketchup. And they actually come with a jar of sauce.
• Porcelain currywurst plates, kpm-berlin.com

Books

Alone in Berlin
• Hans Fallada, 1947

Wrestling with his conscience after a complicated relationship with the Nazi regime, the troubled, prolific German writer wrote his masterpiece while in an insane asylum—and died very soon after. The novel is a psychological epic, swooping into the brains of several day-to-day characters living in the paranoid nightmare that was Hitler's Berlin.

Axolotl Roadkill
• Helene Hegemann, 2010

A coming-of-age story, Berlin-style: 16-year-old Mifti, diagnosed as a "pseudo stress-debilitated" child, loses herself in the city's rave scene. The author was just 18 when the book was published, establishing her as the new wunderkind of the German literary scene. "Der Spiegel" wrote: "Such a debut is very rare... a masterfully narrated surrealism."

The Beauty of Transgression
• Danielle de Picciotto, 2011

Berlin wasn't always this cool. It used to be even cooler. Satisfy your fly-on-the-wall fantasies with this personal memoir by someone who was around to see just how wild, free and beautiful the city was before, during and after the fall of the Wall. Multitalented, multidisciplinary artist De Picciotto was born in the US before her life-defining move to West Berlin in 1987.

Films

Victoria
• Sebastian Schipper, 2015

A Spanish girl falls in with rough, charming street characters, and it all unfolds—and unravels—from there. Famously shot in one continuous take, this thrilling heist movie has everything you'd expect from a Berlin nocturnal adventure.

Just a Gigolo
• David Hemmings, 1978

A WWI veteran works in a Berlin brothel run by a baroness. This black comedy has a killer cast—David Bowie, Kim Novak, and Marlene Dietrich in her last film role. Yet, despite being Germany's most expensive film at the time, it's largely been forgotten.

People on Sunday
• Robert Siodmak & Edgar G. Ulmer, 1930

Subtitled "a film without actors", this influential silent movie presents a snapshot of peaceful innocence in pre-Hitler Berlin. A whimsical tale of ordinary people spending and misspending their precious day off.

Music

Tangerine Dream
• Electronic Meditation, 1970

From Dalí to Hendrix and Stockhausen, the list of TD's influences is long and varied. And this, the album that came long before they settled into New Wave soundtracks, is a perfectly surreal and psychedelic homage to them all.

Basic Channel
• Quadrant Dub, 1993

This holy grail of techno oeuvres marked the beginning of Moritz von Oswald and Mark Ernestus's prolific musical journey together. It also happened to change the course of club music history. Birds of a feather...

Einstürzende Neubauten
• Perpetuum Mobile, 2004

Over 20 years later, Blixa Bargeld and company have still got it. "It" might not be the seething violent energy of the band's first musical forays—but something just as impressive is to be found in this quieter expression.

Some trips are too short for bad meals.

Make sure they're all good with the LOST iN app.

Download on the
App Store

GET IT ON
Google Play

AMANO Group

If it's a neighbourhood worth exploring, you can bet AMANO's got a place for you to stay. With five locations across Berlin, these lifestyle boutique hotels offer guests top-notch urban dwelling options at reasonable price points, as well as the kind of stand-out restaurants and bars you'd expect to find in the buzzing bohemian capital. And it's not just hype—classy design, the kind of service you seldom see in Berlin and all types of creature comforts round out the offer. The only problem is which one to choose.

Hotel AMANO, Auguststraße 43, AMANO Grand Central, Heidestrasse 62
AMANO Home, Torstrasse 52, Hotel MANI, Torstrasse 136
Hotel ZOE, Grosse Präsidentenstr. 6-7

Book now at www.amanogroup.de

Wavejumpers

MOONER MARJANOVIC

On 24 November 1994, at approximately three o'clock CET, the Schumann resonance value reached 62 hertz in the Japanese town of Moshiri for the first time since the measurement method had been rediscovered at the start of the 1990s.

Meanwhile, in the vaults of a former bank on the former death strip that had divided Berlin five years earlier, this passed without a trace; at least not for Kurt, and at least not yet. The bass tones rolled, the hi-hat tweeted, and in the strobe storm he was busy making his way through the crowd after a two-vodka breakfast. It was never a good idea to get up in the middle of the night to burn through the morning hours in the techno clubs. Everyone else in the club was already full on—only Kurt emerged fresh from his dreams, awoken by two women who insisted on taking him out at three in the morning. By the time he made it to the cloakroom, he'd already lost them, but as they say, "in for a penny, in for a pound"—and Kurt was always one for going all in. Struggling, seeking sustenance, searching for an awakening, he ran into Max's arms. Max pressed a glass into his hand and said "The hammer in your head's going boom boom boom," grinning broadly before disappearing into the fog. After the water, Kurt felt better and went with the flow of the crowd.

Sixteen hours later, his mouth dry, Kurt's heart was beating irregularly—more drum 'n' bass than techno. It was cold this afternoon at Dennewitz on the corner of Potsdamer Street. The kebab stall promised a cold Coke at least. He looked down at his hands. That wasn't dirt on his over-long nails; it was an earthy, dark red. The dull colour of congealed blood covered the back of his right hand and all the way to his elbow. The earth vibrated. "Should I call an ambulance?" asked the Turkish man behind the mirrored counter. Kurt shook his head; he couldn't find any wounds, he felt no pain.

Flashback: the Lebanese café near Moabit Prison. That was where he always bought his hash. You sat down, waited at the table, and they took your order. Someone else brought the goods—that's how it worked: 24/7, Berlin style. Just not this time. He only wanted to leave the club for a moment, but the delivery simply never came. Instead, Kurt had to share his table with a tall, thin guy in his early twenties. He wanted to involve Kurt in a conversation, no matter what. The dark-haired dude with a flickering gaze introduced himself, in a pronounced Hessian accent: "Hey, my name is Nenad." There are some people who simply cannot stand silences—in the lift or at the drug dealer's. Inevitably, a game of backgammon broke out. The entry fee was five marks. Kurt lost, listlessly. "Don't worry about it, I always win," grinned Nenad. "I'm saving it for my horoscope computer, then I can work out what lies in your future. But that costs extra." Kurt could barely concentrate on a conversation. Angel definitely wouldn't wait, but the next sentence woke him up like a cold slap to the face: "I started smoking in juvie.

Three years ago. Killed my father with a stone." At that moment, two baggies with three grams of black Afghan were delivered to them at the table. Kurt nodded to Nenad, avoided touching anything, and crept into the open air.

Snake came from the former east of the city. He was an icon in the clubs, a tattooed giant. He had the right stuff, knew the hottest women, and everyone was in love with his muscled body. Snake, however, was more interested in boys. The hot Hungarian was there again tonight with his clique. As she headed directly for him in her black leather jumpsuit, Kurt clung to a metal beam on the shaky bar. "Hi, I'm Angel," she said, and without waiting for an answer, she licked him with her wet tongue on his right bicep, up to the shoulder, where his cut-off denim jacket covered his skin. Snake called over: "Fuck that horny bitch right here. Do it on the counter—for us." Kurt was glad that he immediately turned back to one of his boys. Drexciya's "Wavejumper" was blasting out of the speakers. Perhaps he could still make something out of this fractured morning after all.

A typical dealer's apartment. Scales on the wooden table, packets in aluminium foil, razor blades. The white sun beat down through the holes in the old bedsheets that hung in front of the window as curtains. The bright cones of light above the blue-painted wooden floor illuminated the endless dance of fibres, lint, and pollen. Sandy waves rolled over the unpapered walls. Kurt was naked. His hard cock seemed like a tool, not part of him, with a mechanical hoeing motion, chop, chop, Angel moaned. Then a deep dive. No sense of time, but he had already left his body in that cave. She was still a quivering bundle of flesh as he observed their two bodies from above and saw all the blood—on the sheets, his stomach, and his face. Someone was hammering on the door.

Only once Kurt reached his small apartment on Bergmannstrasse did he feel safe. The vibration flattened out, the taste of onions in his mouth settled. The light on the answering machine was flashing. Kurt hesitated. Once the frequency of the flashing red dot had synchronised with his heartbeat, he finally pressed play. It was Max. "Hey dude, you OK? I hope you didn't come down too quickly. 300 milligrams of Sunshine is really going for it. We're going to Walfisch now. Motte is putting on a special set. You're on the list. Show up." Another Sunday scene, while in Moshiri, the third shift was already starting up.

Zoran "Mooner" Marjanovic lived as a writer in Berlin from 1986–1996. He moved to Goa in the late 1990s, but disappeared soon after. His former roommate and partner Annette Pate found this and other writings in a box.

an Niclaus

Available from LOST iN

And many more cities in the LOST iN Mobile App

LOSTIN.COM